Black on White
and Read All Over

THE STORY OF PRINTING

Black on White and Read All Over

THE STORY OF PRINTING

by ALBERT BARKER

Illustrated by Anthony D'Adamo

and with photographs

JULIAN MESSNER NEW YORK

Published by Julian Messner, a Division of Simon & Schuster, Inc.,
1 West 39 Street, New York, N.Y. 10018. All rights reserved.

Copyright, ©, 1971 by Albert Barker

Printed in the United States of America
ISBN 0-671-32393-8 Cloth Trade
0-671-32394-6 MCE
Library of Congress Catalog Card No. 77-141835
Design: Marjorie Zaum K.

Photo Credits
Boise Cascade Papers: 49, 60 (top), 62
Halliday Lithograph Corporation: 50, 51, 52, 53
Leon Kotkofsky: 80
New York Public Library Picture Collection: 14, 21, 25, 35
Vail-Ballou Press, Inc.: 79 (bottom), 81, 82
Western Collection, Denver Public Library: 40, 41

Contents

CHAPTER I

China's Two Secrets

Suppose you woke up one morning and discovered that there were no newspapers! Not a single book or magazine, no shopping bags, no tickets, no labels, cardboard boxes, no paper money—nothing made of paper!

Can you imagine a world without paper? How could a school or a business or a government get along without paper? Without typewritten pages to read from, radio and television people would not know what to broadcast. Paper is needed in so many places we never think about. For instance, paper is used inside certain electric wires. If the paper is gone, there can be no electric light or power.

You will probably think of other problems that might happen if there was no paper.

If you had lived 2000 years ago in China, the lack of paper wouldn't have bothered you. You would have written your lessons on strips of bamboo or blocks of wood with a bamboo pen dipped in ink made from tree sap. Sometimes you might write a letter on silk. But silk was expensive and wood was too heavy.

One day in the year A.D. 105, a Chinese servant named Ts'ai Lun got tired of carrying his master's heavy wooden blocks. He thought, if only I can make something that is light and strong and cheap that my master can write on, it will make my burden easier.

Ts'ai Lun noticed that old rags and fish nets were made out of tiny fibers—thousands of fine threadlike strings. Looking closely at the bark of mulberry trees and hemp plants, he could see more fibers. These tiny fibers gave him an idea.

Taking the rags, nets, bark and hemp, he dumped them into a kettle of boiling water. As they boiled, he pounded them to separate the fibers. When nothing remained but a thick soupy liquid, he poured it onto a flat screen. The thousands of fibers spread out across the top of the screen. Then he pressed the water out, and when the sun had dried the fibers, they formed a thick rough sheet that could be written on.

At last, Ts'ai Lun had found a way to make his burden lighter! This was the first step in China's papermaking process. For many years, the Chinese were able to keep papermaking a secret.

But they didn't know that in another part of the world, the Egyptians had been making their own kind of "paper" as far back as 3000 B.C. The Egyptians used the papyrus reed that grew along the Nile River. The word *paper* comes from papyrus, but it is not true paper, such as the page of this book.

The Chinese, however, were not satisfied just to write on their paper; they wanted to find a way to *print* on it.

The need for printing arose because handlettering was a slow, tedious, and costly process. Printing would be faster and cheaper. Mainly, it would be a way to make many copies from one original piece of writing. To make copies from an original is to reproduce the original. Printing, therefore, is a method of reproduction. Making copies, or reproductions, very quickly is

Ts'ai noticed that old rags, mulberry bark, fish nets, and hemp plants were made out of tiny fibers. These tiny fibers gave him an idea. He took all these things, dumped them into boiling water, and pounded them to separate the fibers. He poured the soupy,

the main purpose of printing.

Experimenting with small wooden blocks, the Chinese carved designs on one side. In order for the blocks to print, the raised surface of the designs would receive the ink; the cut-away areas would not. But they needed ink to print the designs. So they burned oil and

fibrous liquid onto a flat screen, drained the water off and let the fibers dry in the sun. When they dried, the fibers had formed a thick, rough sheet that could be written on.

covered the black oil smoke with an iron saucer. When the saucer was coated with soot, they scraped the soot off and mixed it with tree sap. This black paste-like ink was smeared on the raised surface of the design which was carved out of the wood block. Then the block was pressed down on the paper. This kind of printing is called *relief printing* or *letterpress*. It means the surfaces that receive ink and transfer the ink to the paper are raised, while the surrounding nonprinting areas are lower.

Printing with blocks was clumsy and slow, so the Chinese looked for a faster way to print. They took soft clay and carved a letter or symbol on it. Then they baked the clay until it was hard. They made hundreds of these clay letters, which could be arranged to form a word or a sentence. After these clay letters were inked, paper was pressed down on them. These carved letters are called *type*, a word meaning "impression." Because this type could be rearranged and used over and over again it is called *movable type*. However, the Chinese language is made up of over forty thousand different letters or signs. Even though the clay type could be moved, the work of printing a single Chinese book often took many months to complete.

Of course, these two secrets—papermaking and movable type—could not remain hidden forever. By the sixth century A.D., Arab traders were able to smuggle samples of paper and type into other Asian countries. Eventually in the year 1150 these Chinese secrets reached Europe by way of Spain.

When you cut shapes out of a bar of soap, you make a raised surface. This raised surface in letter form appeared on Chinese wood blocks and on their movable clay type.

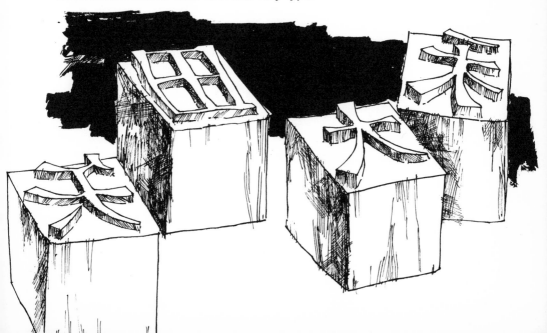

All along the way, each country improved the process of papermaking. But the use of movable type did not succeed in the Asian lands. The Asians preferred the handmade blocks. This carving of letters and designs was considered a fine art, and Asian scholars cherished their books because each one was specially created by a master teacher and carried the only correct and authentic text.

In Europe, only church officials, royal families, and a few rich merchants could read or write. Now, with the two Chinese inventions at hand, it was possible to print books that would teach many people to read.

Chinese printing from the 9th century.

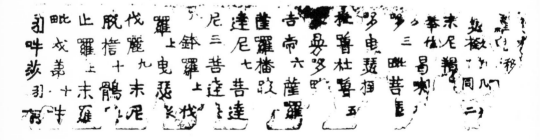

They could learn from books about new things in the world. But paper was very expensive and there were almost no printers. Most books were a series of simple pictures so everyone could understand them, but only the rich could afford to buy them.

What was needed was a quicker, cheaper way to print so that more people could have books. But that quicker, cheaper way was a long time in coming. Over a thousand years passed from the time of Ts'ai Lun's invention to the time of Johann Gaensfleisch in the 1400s. And who was this man? History knows him best as Johann Gutenberg, "The Father of Printing."

CHAPTER 2

Johann Gutenberg's Secret

Books and documents were being printed in Europe before Gutenberg was born in Mainz, Germany, in 1398. After his father died, young Johann Gaensfleisch took his mother's name, Gutenberg, which means Good Mountain.

The boy went to work for a goldsmith and soon learned to carve and stamp designs on metal. In his spare time, he would go to a nearby papermaking factory and watch the men at work. He was fascinated with the idea of printing.

Knowing how to melt gold, silver, lead, and copper started him thinking about making single metal letters and placing them side by side to form words. He knew, of course, that movable type had been used for centuries. In Europe, this type was made of clay. It was uneven in size, it broke easily, it could not hold ink, and using it again and again became a slow, confusing job.

What Gutenberg wanted to make was a metal type with each piece exactly the same size (such as you see on this page.) He also wanted a quick way to make the type.

To turn his idea into a useful invention required men, money, and tools. He would also need a place where he could carry on his experiments secretly, for in those days there were no laws to protect him if his ideas were stolen.

How was he going to make tiny pieces of type? How was he going to make all the letters of the German alphabet so that each tiny letter would fit evenly against the next letter?

Here is what he did:

He took two L-shaped pieces of iron shaped like this ⌐_⌐ . These would slide together like this ⌐_⌐ to form a hollow cavity called a *mold*. Then he took a tiny square of soft metal. With a small steel nail, he carefully tapped the shape of the letter into the metal. Next he dropped this letter into the mold. Now he poured hot lead or tin into the mold. When the metal had cooled and hardened, he lifted it out of the mold. He held in his hand a small neatly shaped piece of type with a raised letter on one end.

Sounds simple, doesn't it? But he had to make many exact copies of each letter. The L-shaped pieces in which Gutenberg made his type are called an *adjustable type mold*, because they can be adjusted to fit all letters of different width, such as an I and a W.

Arranging the type and spelling out words and sentences, Gutenberg soon had an entire page of type. He fastened the pieces of type together tightly, spread ink over the type, and then pressed a sheet of paper down on the coated letters. This kind of printing is called *letterpress*, today.

There was trouble, however. The ink that was used on type made of wood would not stick on the metal type. After many experiments, he found a way to mix Chinese lamp black, a kind of paint, with oil.

Now that Gutenberg had the movable metal type and the right kind of ink, he was ready to print his first book. But he needed some kind of a machine that would press the paper firmly down on the inked type so that he would get a good black impression. Because Ger-

Here Gutenberg is "pulling" his first proof from movable type.

many was a winemaking country, Gutenberg was able to buy a winepress which he moved into his shop. A winepress is used to squeeze the juice out of grapes. Gutenberg made a few changes, and soon his hand-operated press began to turn out printed pages, one at a time.

His first book was a Latin grammar, but his great ambition was to print copies of the Bible in Latin. He knew this work would cost more money than he had. He would need several presses, many sheets of vellum (calfskin) for Bible covers, a big supply of paper, a lot more type, and money to pay the men who would work in his printshop.

Johann Gutenberg was not a good businessman. A wealthy goldsmith named Fust loaned him the needed money and made him sign several legal papers. However, Gutenberg was unable to pay his debt. Before long, Fust and a friend took over the shop and equipment.

Gutenberg lost everything except two hundred

Gutenberg probably used a press similar to this one on which to print his first book.

20

copies of the Bible he had printed. Discouraged and almost penniless, Gutenberg sold these precious Bibles to German monasteries for whatever he could get. Today only twelve of the Bibles remain. One of them is in the Library of Congress in Washington and is valued at $200,000.

Eventually a new ruler came to Mainz. Hearing about the Bibles and the great work this Mainz printer had done, the ruler granted Johann Gutenberg a small

A page from one of Gutenberg's books.

pension. It was a reward for "the grateful and willing service rendered, and that he may still render in the future."

Johann Gutenberg never did any more printing after his trouble with Fust. He did not realize that his simple little invention—the adjustable type mold, and his use of a press for bringing the inked metal and paper firmly together—would have a great effect on printing throughout Europe.

When Gutenberg died at the age of seventy-one, printing shops had opened in Italy, Holland, Belgium, and France. Hundreds of printers journeyed across Europe. Many carried their type and equipment on their back. In every village, they found the people eager to read. These journeyman printers produced all kinds of books—everything from Greek classics to books on arithmetic.

By the time Columbus discovered America in 1492, almost 40,000 different kinds of books had been printed in Europe. There were hundreds of copies of each kind of book, so it is estimated that 20 million books were being read.

The printed word began to change people's lives.

For the first time, facts and stories could be written down. The word of mouth and storytelling that formed the oral tradition of learning was no longer necessary. It was replaced by a body of recorded knowledge that grew with each printed book. As long as these printed books were preserved, the wisdom and knowledge of past poets, historians, and scientists were available to everyone. As people increased their own knowledge, or added to the body of recorded knowledge, civilization advanced more rapidly than anyone ever dreamed possible.

CHAPTER 3

Printing Comes to England

The first printed book in the English language was not printed in England but in Bruges, a city in Belgium. A wealthy cloth merchant, William Caxton, went there on business in 1474, and became enthusiastic over the possibilities of printing books in English. But there was no English type, so Caxton had to do as Gutenberg did earlier. He had to make his own type.

Caxton opened a printing shop in London near Westminster Abbey. He was more interested in what went *on* the pages of his books than in their appearance. He knew that although the English language was spoken, there was no accepted way of spelling certain words. So he began to standardize the words. First he would translate foreign books into English, spelling out many new words. In this way, he made it possible for all English-speaking people to read, understand, and speak the same language. Today, thanks to Caxton's early work, every book or newspaper printed in English can be understood in Canada, New York, New Zealand, Australia, or wherever English is spoken.

However, one problem bothered all printers everywhere. Although the type they used was metal and movable, there were no standard sizes. This printer would make his own type of one size. That printer made another size. The next printer bought some type from

An English print shop in 1619.

a neighboring printer, but it was larger or smaller. The results were printed pages with the type sizes all mixed, capital letters in the wrong place, periods missing.

In France, these complications led to so much confusion that a Paris typemaker, Pierre Fournier, attempted to standardize all type sizes. He made up a scale that would regulate the size and height of type. In this way, all printers would be able to make or buy type that would print uniformly. A royal decree was issued in 1723, commanding all printers to follow Fournier's scale, but nobody paid any attention to the decree.

About 1775, a printer by the name of Didot took Fournier's system and improved on it. Today printers call it the *point system*. It is still used, but there have been many changes.

Let's see how this system operates today.

Type size is measured in points, 72 points equal 1 inch. Thus, an 8-point type would be cast on a piece of metal whose height is 8/72 of an inch.

(The type you are reading is 14 point.)

Naturally, the size and style of type a printer uses will depend on what is to be printed, the kind of paper, and the cost. For example, 8-point type takes up less space than 10- or 12-point type, and uses less paper.

Type is set side by side in long or short lines. The length of a line of type is measured in *picas*. One pica measures 1/6 of an inch.

(The lines in this book are 24 picas long.)

Today, all printers use the point system and guess-work is eliminated. Yet just 300 years ago, printers were still making their own type in many odd shapes and sizes.

In England at the beginning of the eighteenth century, a young engraver, William Caslon, decided he would make or cut type and sell it to printers. By 1720 he had started a *foundry*, a special kind of factory where things are made of melted metal. *Foundry type* is a single letter made of hard metal and used when setting type by hand.

Caslon designed his own style letters, and then made up a sample page showing what his type foundry could make. Almost immediately, printers from all over England bought his type. It was so popular that Benjamin Franklin arranged for the Declaration of Independence to be set in Caslon type.

wm. CAsloN dDQ 1692 1766 SS, JULY 4, 1776. Declaration of the thi—

William Caslon, a young engraver, designed a style of type that became so popular that Benjamin Franklin arranged for the Declaration of Independence to be set in Caslon type.

Caslon type is still used today. In fact, this book is printed in a type face called "Caslon."

In contrast to Caslon was John Baskerville, who started his English printing shop about 1750. Where Caslon was interested in the contents of his books, Baskerville was more interested in making books that looked beautiful. He wanted everything to be perfect—the press, the paper, and ink, which he made himself. Then he designed his own alphabet shapes from A to Z.

(This is 18 point Baskerville.)

All this careful work cost a lot of time and money, but Baskerville was a rich man and printing was his way of having fun. It took him seven years to get ready to print his first book. It was the work of a Roman poet, Vergil, and when the book finally appeared, it was praised all through Europe. Many people thought it was too elaborate and called Baskerville a clever but wasteful amateur.

Baskerville didn't care. He was determined to print the most beautiful volume of the Holy Bible in all the world. It took him six years to do this. The book was beautiful, but it was expensive. Out of the 1,250 copies printed, only half were sold. People could not afford to buy it.

However, more important than Baskerville's printing of beautiful books was his influence on printing, particularly in Europe where his type designs were praised. The French copied his clean, sharp letters; the Italians imitated his bold, distinctive pages.

John Baskerville died in the year 1775. By that time his name was well known among the printers in the Thirteen Colonies.

But printing had come to the New World long before the Colonists fought the War for Independence.

CHAPTER 4

Printing Crosses
the Atlantic

Who brought the first printing press to the New World? Many students of history have tried to answer that question. We do know that there was a young Italian named Juan Pablos who worked in a printing shop in Seville, Spain. One day in the year 1539 his master asked him to set up a press in Mexico City. At this time, Mexico was a Spanish colony. The Spanish Archbishop of Mexico wanted someone to print religious books in the native Indian languages for the priests and missionaries.

Juan Pablos arrived in Mexico City with his young wife and two assistants, both Spaniards, one a black. With this small group, he began to print books for the Indians. After a few years, he was able to add another press and make his own type. Only a few precious pages remain today to show his pioneer work.

Spain had other colonies in the New World, and the printing press was introduced to remote parts of South America. This was a hundred years before printing came to North America.

The Pilgrims arrived at Plymouth Rock in 1620. But it took eighteen more years before the printing press arrived in the Massachusetts Bay Colony.

The American colonists were beginning to take an interest in education. They started schools and planned to establish a college. When José Glover, a minister, discovered there were no textbooks, he bought a press, supplies of paper, ink, and type in England. He hired Stephen Daye and his two sons to go with him overseas. On the return trip, José Glover died, but he can be regarded as the father of printing in the United States.

The Dayes, father and sons, carried on the work. Their first piece of printing was "The Freeman's Oath," which was printed on a half-sheet of small paper. Not a single copy remains today.

Then came the first book, known as the *Bay Psalm*

Book. There are ten copies of this book in existence, and they are poorly printed. Nevertheless if a complete copy should ever be offered for sale, it would bring a fabulous sum of money. One copy of the *Bay Psalm Book* was bought by the New York Public Library for $151,000.

The desire to print the Bible was as strong in the Colonies as it had been in England and in Europe. And so a master printer by the name of Johnson left London for New England. In Boston he began working on the Bible with Samuel Green, who now owned the Daye printshop. This was the first *edition* of the Scriptures in any language to be printed in North America. Johnson also printed a Bible for the Indians. In those days, to translate Indian sounds into print was almost impossible. Nevertheless, the Colonists were determined to win the Indians over to Christianity by teaching them to read from their own version of the Bible.

The Colonies began to grow as hundreds of emigrants arrived from England and Europe. Soon new settlements appeared, and some of these villages became towns. At the mouth of the Hudson River an island was being settled by the Dutch. They called it New Amsterdam, but the British renamed it New York. And in the Province of Pennsylvania on the Delaware River, there was the new community called Philadelphia.

The citizens of these towns wanted to know what was going on. They needed newspapers, and newspapers needed men to print them.

One of these men became famous as a patriot, statesman, diplomat, and scientist. He was a signer of the Declaration of Independence and the most distinguished citizen of his time. But first of all, he considered himself a printer.

As a boy of twelve, Ben Franklin worked in the printshop of his half-brother, James, in Boston. James also published one of the earliest Colonial newspapers, *The New England Courant*. At first, Ben did only chores. As time went by, he learned how to set type and operate a press. When James printed something in his newspaper that the authorities didn't like, they closed his shop. Then James got an idea: he would issue the paper under the name of his younger brother.

Thus, in 1723, *The New England Courant* was published with this notice: "*Boston: Printed and sold by Benjamin Franklin in Queen Street, where Advertisements are taken in.*"

But young Ben and James couldn't get along, so

THE
New-England Courant.

From MONDAY February 4. to MONDAY February 11. 1723.

The late Publisher of this Paper, finding so many Inconveniencies would arise by his carrying the Manuscripts and publick News to be supervis'd by the Secretary, as to render his carrying it on unprofitable, has intirely dropt the Undertaking. The present Publisher having receiv'd the following Piece, desires the Readers to accept of it as a Preface to what they may hereafter meet with in this Paper.

Non ego mordaci distrinxi Carmine quenquam.
Nulla venenato Litera mista Joco est.

LONG has the Press groaned in bringing forth an hateful, but numerous Brood of Party Pamphlets, malicious Scribbles, and Billingsgate Ribaldry. The Rancour and bitterness it has unhappily infused into Mens minds, and to what a Degree it has soured and leaven'd the Tempers of Persons formerly esteemed some of the most sweet and affable, is too well known here, to need any further Proof or Representation of the Matter.

No generous and impartial Person then can blame the present Undertaking, which is designed purely for the Diversion and Merriment of the Reader. Pieces of Pleasancy and Mirth have a secret Charm in them to allay the Heats and Tumors of our Spirits, and to make a Man forget his restless Resentments. They have a strange Power to tune the harsh Disorders of the Soul, and reduce us to a serene and placid State of Mind.

The main Design of this Weekly Paper will be to entertain the Town with the most comical and diverting Incidents of Humane Life, which in so large a Place as Boston, will not fail of a universal Exemplification: Nor shall we be wanting to fill up these Papers with a grateful Interspersion of more serious Morals, which may be drawn from the most ludicrous and odd Parts of Life.

As for the Author, that is the next Question. But tho' we profess our selves ready to oblige the ingenious and courteous Reader with most Sorts of Intelligence, yet here we beg a Reserve. Nor will it be of any Manner of Advantage either to them or to the Writers, that their Names should be published; and therefore in this Matter we desire the Favour of you to suffer us to hold our Tongues: Which tho' at this Time of Day it may sound like a very uncommon Request, yet it proceeds from the very Hearts of your Humble Servants.

By this Time the Reader perceives that more than one are engaged in the present Undertaking. Yet is there one Person, an Inhabitant of this Town of Boston, whom we honour as a Doctor in the Chair, or a perpetual Dictator.

The Society had design'd to present the Publick with his Effigies, but that the Limner, to whom he was presented for a Draught of his Countenance, descryed (and this he is ready to offer upon Oath) Nineteen Features in his Face, more than ever he beheld in any Humane Visage before; which so raised the Price of his Picture, that our Master himself forbid the Extravagance of coming up to it. And then besides, the Limner objected a Schism in his Face, which splits it from his Forehead in a strait Line down to his Chin, in such sort, that Mr. Painter protests it is a double Face, and he'll have Four Pounds for the Pourtraiture. However, tho' this double Face has spoilt us of a pretty Picture, yet we all rejoiced to see old Janus in our Company.

There is no Man in Boston better qualified than old Janus for a Couranteer, or if you please, an Observator, being a Man of such remarkable Opticks, as to look two ways at once.

As for his Morals, he is a cheasty Christian, as the Country Phrase expresses it. A Man of good Temper, courteous Deportment, sound Judgment; a mortal Hater of Nonsense, Foppery, Formality, and endless Ceremony.

As for his Club, they aim at no greater Happiness or Honour, than the Publick be made to know; that it is the utmost of their Ambition to attend upon and do all imaginable good Offices to good Old Janus the Couranteer, who is and always will be the Readers humble Servant.

P. S. Gentle Readers, we design never to let a Paper pass without a Latin Motto if we can possibly pick one up, which carries a Charm in it to the Vulgar, and the learned admire the pleasure of Construing. We should have obliged the World with a Greek Scrap or two, but the Printer has no Types, and therefore we Intreat the candid Reader not to Impute the defect to our Ignorance, for our Doctor can say all the Greek Letters by heart.

His Majesty's Speech to the Parliament, October 11. tho' already publish'd, may perhaps be new to many of our Country Readers; we shall therefore insert it in this Day's Paper.

His MAJESTY's most Gracious SPEECH to both Houses of Parliament, on Thursday October 11. 1722.

My Lords and Gentlemen,

I Am sorry to find my self obliged, at the Opening of this Parliament, to acquaint you, That a dangerous Conspiracy has been for some time formed, and is still carrying on against my Person and Government, in Favour of a Popish Pretender.

The Discoveries I have made here, the Informations I have received from my Ministers abroad, and the Intelligences I have had from the Powers in Alliance with me, and indeed from most parts of Europe, have given me most ample and current Proofs of this wicked Design.

The Conspirators have, by their Emissaries, made the strongest Instances for Assistance from Foreign Powers, but were disappointed in their Expectations: However, confiding in their Numbers, and not discouraged by their former ill Success, they resolved once more, upon their own strength, to attempt the subversion of my Government.

To this End they provided considerable Sums of Money, engaged great Numbers of Officers from abroad, secured large Quantities of Arms and Ammunition, and thought themselves in such Readiness; that had not the Conspiracy been timely discovered, we should, without doubt, before now have seen the whole Nation, and particularly the City of London, involved in Blood and Confusion.

The Care I have taken has, by the Blessing of God, hitherto prevented the Execution of their trayterous Projects. The Troops have been incamped all this Summer; six Regiments (though very necessary for the Security of that Kingdom) have been brought over from Ireland; The States General have given me assurances that they would keep a considerable Body of Forces in readiness to give such assistance No

A front page from James Franklin's newspaper, *The New England Courant,* one of the earliest published in the Colonies.

Ben went to New York looking for a job, and then to Philadelphia. There he found a job as a printer's helper. As the years went by, he improved his skill as a printer. At the age of twenty, he bought a printing shop and started a newspaper, *The Pennsylvania Gazette*.

Franklin also wanted to write and publish an almanac. It would show the days and months of the year, special holidays, and when the moon would be

At the age of twenty, Benjamin Franklin bought a small printing shop. Soon he was publishing *The Pennsylvania Gazette,* and a popular book of sayings, proverbs, advice and information called *Poor Richard's Almanac.*

new, full, and in the first and last quarter. The little almanac would include advice on cooking, farming, health, poems, wise sayings, and other kinds of useful information.

When Franklin printed this booklet in 1758, he didn't use his own name as the writer. He remembered that a printer in England by the name of Richard Saunders had published *Richard's Almanac,* so Franklin decided to call his American almanac *Poor Richard's.* It was printed each year and was very popular in the Colonies. Many of "Poor Richard's" sayings are still used today. Here are a few you may be familiar with:

"Early to bed, Early to rise, makes a Man healthy, wealthy and wise."

"A cat in gloves catches no mice."

"God helps Them that help Themselves."

"Diligence is the mother of Good Luck."

During the Colonial period, another printer was to become an important part of our history when he fought for freedom of the press.

The Colonies, which still belonged to England,

had strict laws concerning what a printer could and could not publish. In 1735, a German emigrant printer named John Peter Zenger was arrested for publishing articles in his newspaper, *The New York Weekly Journal*. These articles disagreed with the actions of the governor of the New York colony. He declared Zenger had broken the law. Andrew Hamilton, the lawyer who defended the printer, was a friend of

In 1735, John Peter Zenger fought a famous court battle for freedom of the press. Later, freedom of the press became an important principle of American democracy and was written into the Constitution of the United States.

Benjamin Franklin's. Hamilton argued that Zenger had merely printed the truth. He asked the jury to decide not just whether Zenger had broken the law, but whether truth or falsehood had been printed.

The jury decided in favor of Zenger. This was a famous victory, for now a printer was free to print the facts, no matter how unpleasant they might be to some people. Freedom of the press was later written into the Constitution of the United States, and is one of the most important principles of American democracy.

The spread of printing in the Colonies was interrupted by the American Revolution. After independence was won, a vast area of land opened beyond the Allegheny Mountains, and a great move westward began.

Fired by the pioneering spirit, printers joined the settlers moving into new, unexplored parts of the country. They opened up printing shops in the one-street villages. Often their only news came from travelers heading into the western wilderness or returning to the civilized East. They printed single-sheet newspapers, posters that offered rewards for robbers, handbills that advertised land for sale, and crude maps of explored territory.

In 1859, *The Rocky Mountain Press,* Colorado's first newspaper, was set up in the loft of a Denver store. Its editors, type setters, and apprentices worked with their firearms handy. Outlaws knew that the coming of the press was a sure sign that law and order would soon follow.

From these pioneer printers, travelers knew what dangers were ahead. They learned useful facts, had maps and traveling information that saved time, money, and lives. These printers and their tools—printing press, type, ink, and paper—side by side with the settler's Bible, axe, and plow, played a vital part in the development of the American West.

Pioneer presses often printed wanted posters like this one offering a $5,000 reward for the capture of "Billy the Kid"—dead or alive!

CHAPTER 5

=〕0▭〕0▭〕0▭〕0▭〕0▭〕0▭〕0▭〕0▭〕0▭〕0▭〕0

The Discovery
of Lithography

=〕0▭〕0▭〕0▭〕0▭〕0▭〕0▭〕0▭〕0▭〕0▭〕0▭〕0

For hundreds of years, from the days of Chinese block printing to the days of Gutenberg, and for 350 years more, there had been only one way to print. This was the letterpress method—using raised letters of type that were inked, and then pressing paper down on the type.

Toward the close of the eighteenth century, Alois Senefelder, a young writer and law student in Munich, Germany, accidentally found a new way to print. He had written a play for the town carnival and had had it printed into a booklet. But printing booklets cost more money than Alois could afford. Nor could he afford to buy a printing press and type.

One day in 1793, young Senefelder wanted to make a list of clothes that were to be sent out to be washed. Not having any paper handy, he used a flat wet stone and wrote on it with a greasy crayon made of wax, soap, oil, and lampblack. Later he took a sheet of paper, and just as an experiment, he pressed the paper against the stone. When he pulled it off, there was his laundry list printed, but in reverse. What was SHIRT was now TЯIHꙄ.

After several thousand experiments, Senefelder hit upon a method that was to bring him world fame. Here is how his invention worked:

First, he drew his design on a smooth, flat slab of limestone with a greasy crayon. Then he moistened the stone with water. The water stayed on the stone surface but did not stick to the oily crayon marks.

Then he rolled the stone with a roller soaked in greasy printer's ink. The ink couldn't stick to the wet stone, but it *could* stick to the oily crayon marks.

When he pressed a sheet of paper against the inked stone, the paper picked up ink only from the design he had drawn with the crayon. In this way he printed his original design, in reverse, on paper. He had discovered the simple fact that was to forever change the course of

the printed word: *oil and water do not mix.*

Senefelder called his invention *lithography* from the Greek word *lithos,* meaning stone, and *graph,* which means writing.

Artists were quick to see the advantages of lithography. Now they need make only *one* original drawing upon the stone, ink the stone, and from that stone make many prints which would be copies (though in reverse) of the original *one.* But they discovered something more. They were able to make pictures in black and white as well as in color.

They would draw the same design on several slabs of limestone. Then they would take a sheet of paper and make a first print, perhaps only part of it, in black. On the next stone a different color ink was applied, and the same sheet of paper used. Sometimes an artist would use as many as twelve different colors, and the result was a beautiful picture. Today, in museums, libraries, and in books, you will see copies of lithograph pictures by such famous artists as Dürer, Daumier, Toulouse-Lautrec, Currier and Ives, and even our modern artists.

For a while, stone continued to be the ideal mate-

Alois Senefelder discovered lithography when he ran out of paper on which to write a laundry list and used, instead, a stone.

rial for lithographic printing. But stone is heavy, it is easily damaged, and it is difficult to store for safekeeping. The printing must be done with the stone lying flat. Altogether it is a slow and costly process. So printers were forced to find more practical and faster methods based on the lithographic principle that oil and water do not mix.

Just as an "accident" led to Senefelder's invention of lithography, so did an "accident" lead to offset lithography in 1904.

In Nutley, New Jersey, a printer named Ira Rubel had a simple *rotary press*, which printed single sheets of paper on one side of the sheet only.

Rubel's job was to stand beside the press and feed sheets into the machine one at a time. The paper would slide between the type cylinder and a smooth cylinder underneath, which would press the paper up against the type to make the impression.

One day, Rubel forgot to feed a blank sheet into the busy press. The inked type printed on the smooth second cylinder. Rubel saw his mistake and quickly fed a sheet into the press. This resulted in *two* impressions on the paper: on one side from the type cylinder and on the other side an impresson from the smooth second cylinder. For some reason, which Rubel couldn't understand at the time, the second impression was much cleaner and clearer.

Ira Rubel began to experiment and finally built a three-cylinder press. From his invention comes the *offset lithography* method used today.

The first cylinder holds the curved type plate. As the type plate rotates, it comes into contact with a dampening roller. This dampener wets the plate with water so the nonprinting areas will not take the ink. The plate cylinder rotates again, and this time another roller applies ink to the printing areas of the plate. The inked image is then transferred to a rubber blanket which covers the second cylinder. Paper is fed between the rubber cylinder and the third, or impression, cylinder.

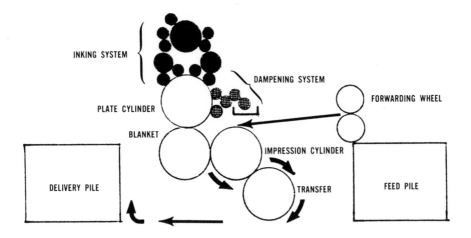

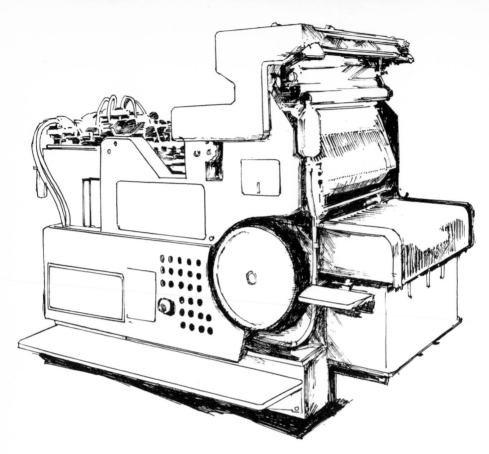

A modern offset lithography press.

It is printed as the rubber cylinder transfers, or "off-sets" the ink to the paper.

Some offset presses print only one side of a sheet; others print both sides of a sheet at one time; still others called *web-fed* presses print on a roll of paper. These web-fed presses can print either only one side of the roll of paper or both sides of the roll at the same time.

Today, about 90 percent of all books are printed by offset lithography. So are magazines, posters, cata-

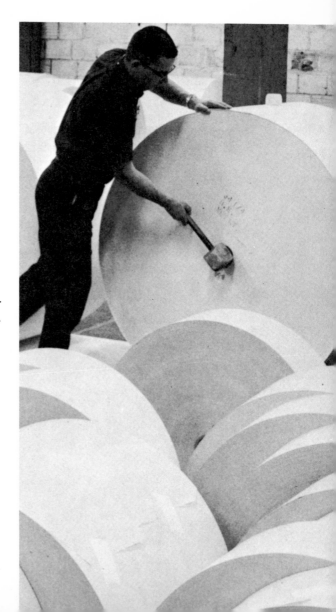

These are rolls of paper that will be used on a web-fed press.

logs, and labels. Even the printing on some tin cans and tubes, such as shaving cream and toothpaste, are printed by offset.

This book, *Black on White and Read All Over,* was printed by offset.

HOW BLACK AND WHITE OFFSET PLATES ARE MADE

When offset lithography (also known as photo-offset printing) is used to print a book, the pages of type and the illustrations must be specially prepared as follows:

First, an expert photographer uses large, special cameras to take pictures of each page. From now on, it is the negatives of these pictures that will be used.

But there was one more printing method yet to be discovered. Gutenberg and the Chinese made letter-press printing possible. Senefelder discovered lithography, and this led to offset lithography.

Now, *rotogravure* was to join the printing family.

Working on a table that is lighted from below, a man takes the negatives of each page and tapes (or strips) them onto a large sheet of paper. This man must be accurate and careful. Besides stripping, his job is to catch and retouch any imperfections on the delicate negatives. The special sheet of paper onto which he strips the negatives is called a flat. One flat can hold as many as sixty-four negatives—enough to print an entire book of sixty-four pages.

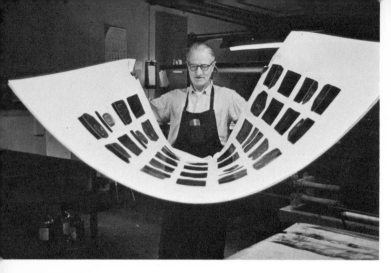

When the negatives of the type and the illustrations have all been taped to the flat, the flat is sent to the offset plate department.

The offset plate department makes an offset plate from a large, thin sheet of aluminum. This sheet of aluminum is placed in an acid solution to clean it. Then running water is used to wash the acid off the aluminum.

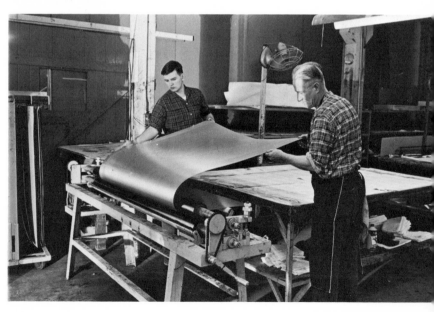

Finally, the aluminum is coated with a chemical that is sensitive to light. The offset plate is now ready for the next step.

The negative flat is fixed tightly against the offset plate, and both are exposed to light. When the light hits the negatives, it prints the negative image onto the offset plate. The plate maker then separates the flat from the plate. Using a sponge or a soft cloth, he coats the plate with a greasy lacquer. This greasy lacquer brings out the exposed areas which are to be printed in black. Next the plate is rinsed in water. Since grease and water do not mix, the printing areas remain black and the non-printing areas will be white.

This is the plate that is placed around the plate cylinder of the offset lithography press. (See pages 47 and 48)

==

CHAPTER 6

Rotogravure
Joins the Family

==

At the time of Gutenberg, artists were engraving or cutting designs directly on copper. They called it *intaglio*, an Italian word meaning to "cut in."

To make a copper engraving, the artist cut his design into the copper sheet or plate with special tools. This was slow work and required a steady hand and keen eyesight.

After the engraver-artist completed his design, he spread the entire plate with ink. Then he carefully wiped the surface so that the only remaining ink was *below the surface*, in the "cut in" design.

The next step was to use a handpress that would force a sheet of paper so tightly against the engraving that the paper would pick up the ink. Sometimes the print would be beautiful. At other times the paper became smeared or failed to pick up the ink. Many printers felt that there must be a better and quicker way to make use of the intaglio method of printing.

Not until 1895, however, did this better way come about. A man named Karl Klic was working for a firm of calico printers in Lancaster, England. Calico is a shiny cotton cloth that is printed with all kinds of colorful designs. Klic had been able to combine photography with copper engraving, and the result was beautiful calico that no other cloth-printing firm could duplicate. Klic called his process *photogravure.* He tried to keep it a secret but failed.

In 1910, Klic's photogravure process was adapted to the rotary printing presses of the *Illustrated London Times.* In looking about for a new word to describe Klic's fine illustrations, the newspaper publisher chose two words. Because the cylinders of the press were round, he took the Latin word *rota,* meaning wheel, and because the copper cylinders were "cut in," he used the French word *gravure,* for engraving. Thus *rotogravure* became a new word in the language of printing.

To make a rotogravure plate or cylinder, a very fine screen is placed over the copper design. Then the metal is "cut in" or *etched* by an acid. This process makes tiny holes, some deeper than others. The deeper holes hold more ink and will, of course, print dark. Where the holes are shallow, the print will be light. If

If you look closely at a rotogravure page of a newspaper, you will see thousands of tiny dots that seem to blend smoothly from light to dark.

you look closely at a rotogravure page, you will see thousands of tiny dots that seem to blend smoothly from light to dark.

Rotogravure is used to print postage stamps, candy wrappers, and the Sunday section in your newspaper. Wallpaper, draperies, dresses, and paper money are also printed this way.

But no matter which printing method is used, printing is simply a way to press letters, words, sentences, and pictures onto a sheet of paper.

That sounds simple enough, doesn't it? However, many years were to pass before type, ink, paper, and presses all came together in what was called the Printing Revolution.

CHAPTER 7

The Printing Revolution

Printed words and pictures became important as people were eager to read anything that would tell them more about the world. Yet it was not until the late 1700s—350 years after Gutenberg's invention—that any important progress was made in the way printing was *done*.

Two things were needed: a machine that would make plenty of cheap paper, and a printing press that would turn out printed pages rapidly. What good was one without the other?

Paper was still being made by hand, sheet by sheet, in a wire mold, much like the Chinese did.

In 1790, a papermaking machine was invented in

Paris by Louis Robert. This was the time of the French Revolution, and nobody in France was interested in the machine. So Robert sold it to two Englishmen by the name of Fourdrinier. They made many improvements in Robert's machine, and even today many papermaking machines are still called "Fourdriniers."

The Fourdrinier papermaking machine was good, but not good enough. Another Englishman, John Dickerson, built a rotary papermaking machine in 1809. With the coming of this improvement, the manufacture of paper increased ten times. Then a new problem arose: there was a shortage of linen rags which had always been used in the making of the best quality paper. The countryside was searched. People sold their linen clothes for high prices. Papermaking factories bought all the fabric that was made of flax. (Linen is made from flax.) But there was not enough linen to keep up with the demand for paper.

Experiments were made with many substitutes: straw, reeds, pine needles, artichoke stems, and the bark of trees. The idea of using pulp, the inner part of wood, had been suggested many years before, but not until 1840 was the process tried.

The final step in the papermaking revolution

An 18th century French paper mill.

As Keller watched his daughter press cherry stones against a wet grindstone, he noticed that the wood broke into small, damp fibers. When he squeezed these fibers, they stuck together, just as the fibers stuck together when Ts'ai Lun had experimented many centuries before. This simple discovery led to Keller's wood-grinding machine.

came in Germany. A weaver named Keller was watching his daughter grind the rough edges of cherry stones to make a string of beads. As she pressed the stones against a wet grindstone with a block of wood, Keller noticed that the inner part of the wood broke into small pieces. He squeezed some of these damp wood fibers between his fingers and saw that they stuck together, just as Ts'ai Lun had noticed many centuries before.

This simple discovery was the beginning of Keller's wood-grinding machine. Eventually, after many improvements, the machine was able to give the world inexpensive paper made from wood pulp. Now paper mills began to use pulp from pine, oak, poplar, and many other trees.

Printers were also trying to build new kinds of printing presses. The old-fashioned handpresses made of wood were constantly wearing out or breaking down. They were also slow: it took nine separate operations to print a single small sheet.

An English Earl, Charles Stanhope, made a handpress out of iron. He reduced the nine separate operations to five, and he increased the size of the press so it could print more type on more paper. The

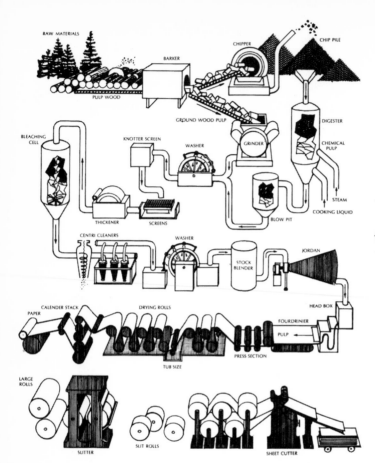

RAW MATERIALS

CHIPPER

CHIP PILE

BARKER

PULP WOOD

GROUND WOOD PULP

DIGESTER

BLEACHING CELL

KNOTTER SCREEN

WASHER

GRINDER

CHEMICAL PULP

STEAM

COOKING LIQUID

THICKENER

SCREENS

BLOW PIT

CENTRI CLEANERS

WASHER

JORDAN

STOCK BLENDER

CALENDER STACK

PAPER

DRYING ROLLS

HEAD BOX

FOURDRINIER

PULP

PRESS SECTION

TUB SIZE

LARGE ROLLS

SLITTER

SLIT ROLLS

SHEET CUTTER

This diagram shows to-day's papermaking process from the raw materials to the finished product.

Stanhope press was considered so fast that many of them were used to print one of England's newspapers, the London *Times*.

By this time, James Watt and others had developed the steam engine. The invention set a young German printer, Frederick Koenig, to thinking. He began to experiment with the idea of applying steam power to the handpress. His invention didn't work very well, and he went to England looking for financial help to continue his work. Newspaper publishers there were anxious to have faster presses, so they gave Koenig money. By 1812, he had built a power-driven cylinder press with an automatic inking system. Now the printing revolution was really under way! The new press could make 800 impressions an hour. But Koenig was not satisfied. He designed a new press that printed 1100 impressions an hour.

And the printing revolution has never stopped. Printing machines have become bigger in size and faster in speed. One kind of press can print 4000 impressions an hour; another can turn out as many as 25,000 impressions an hour. The presses that are the fastest are web-fed.

New and faster presses—better and cheaper paper. But other things were needed in the business of printing. Typemakers (founders) were busy designing new styles in letters.

For several centuries there had been only two type faces: the upright Roman and the black letter Gothic. Now type founding became a separate business,

(This is a Roman style of type.)

(𝕿𝖍𝖎𝖘 𝖎𝖘 𝖆 𝕲𝖔𝖙𝖍𝖎𝖈 𝖇𝖑𝖆𝖈𝖐 𝖑𝖊𝖙𝖙𝖊𝖗 𝖘𝖙𝖞𝖑𝖊 𝖔𝖋 𝖙𝖞𝖕𝖊.)

and printers could have a wide choice of type. They could order a complete assortment of type in one size and style. This assortment is called a *font*, and contains capitals and small letters, numerals, and punctuation marks.

ABCDEFGHIJKLMNOPQRSTUVWXYZ&
ABCDEGMNPTY
ABCDEFGHIJKLMNOPQRSTUVWXYZ
abcdefghijklmnopqrstuvwxyz
1234567890$
,.:;?('!-)'*—

A recent search among printers shows that about 6000 different type faces are available, but only a few are used. People everywhere want simple letters that are easy to read.

Although the printers now had fast presses and fine paper in white and other colors, in sheets and rolls, they were still composing or setting type by hand, letter by letter. The *compositor*, the man who set the type, would stand before a *type case*, which was divided into many small compartments that contained the metal type. The compartments were of different sizes and were arranged somewhat like the letters on a typewriter, with the most-used letters being easiest to reach. For instance, since the letter "e" is used most often, the e's would be in the largest compartment, but the letter "q" would be in a smaller compartment.

Despite these many different-sized compartments, a compositor soon became expert in picking out the correct type. He had to know where each letter was in the type case *without looking,* just as a good typist doesn't have to look at the typewriter keys. Working from left to right, he placed the individual letters side by side in his composing stick. The compositor looks at the letters in the stick upside down and backwards. For example, the word BACKWARD would appear this way in his composing stick— BⱯCKMⱯꓤD—because this is the way it has to be set so that it will print forward.

Working at top speed, his nimble fingers could not set more than 1000 letters an hour. During the

1800s, many books, such as those of the famous English author Charles Dickens, were 200,000 words long. This meant that a compositor had to set more than a million pieces of type.

By 1860, the big newspaper publishers were desperate. Many of them printed their papers or magazines seven days a week. The compositors worked day and night, and this labor alone cost a great deal of money. "Give us a better, quicker way to set type!" the publishers said. They offered huge sums of money to anyone who could build an *automatic* typesetting or composing machine.

Twenty-four years were to pass before such a machine was ready to work. When Thomas Edison, himself a great inventor, saw this machine he called it "the eighth wonder of the world."

Standing before a type case, the compositor selects the individual letters and places them in a metal composing stick which has a slide that can be moved to fit the length of the line to be set. A compositor can set type without looking, just as a good typist doesn't have to look at the typewriter keys.

═❑═❑═❑═❑═❑═❑═❑═❑═❑═❑═❑

CHAPTER 8

The Immigrant Boy
from Württemberg

═❑═❑═❑═❑═❑═❑═❑═❑═❑═❑═❑

Many inventors tried to make an automatic typesetting machine. The newspaper publishers were willing to try them all; but when it came to a severe test, the machines failed.

Among the many inventors was Ottmar Mergenthaler. The people in Württemberg, Germany, where he was born, thought he was very clever with his hands. When their ancient clock in the church tower refused to work, Ottmar climbed up and made the repairs. Here was a twelve-year-old boy who could do what the official clockmaker was unable to do.

Ottmar's cousin had emigrated to Washington, D.C., where he had established an engineering shop. Young Mergenthaler decided the United States was the place for him. When he was eighteen, he joined his cousin. For a while he helped build machines of all kinds, but when he heard about the need for a composing machine, he set to work.

Mergenthaler had very little money, but that didn't stop him from opening a small machine shop. For ten years he worked, building and throwing aside many models that failed. Some newspaper publishers heard of Mergenthaler's attempts to solve the typesetting problem, and they advanced him money so he could continue.

His first machine was demonstrated in the composing room of the *New York Tribune*. The editor, Whitelaw Reid, and other officials watched as Mergenthaler sat at the keyboard of his invention, which looked something like a typewriter. He started the electric motor and began to tap out a sentence. The letters were no longer separate, individual pieces. The machine could set an entire sentence on one long piece of metal.

When Reid saw the result, he said, "Ottmar, you've done it! A line o' type!" And that's how the *Linotype* machine got its name.

This great event, which made possible the modern newspaper, took place in 1886. The advantages of the Linotype were easily seen. Each line of type was brand-new, with perfect printing surfaces. After the type had been used, it was simply melted down and fresh type was made from it. Using a keyboard to set the words was much faster than setting each piece of type by hand.

Mergenthaler's machine saved newspapers thousands of typesetting hours. A man who once set 1000 letters by hand could now set 6000 letters by machine. Today more than 100,000 Linotype machines are in operation throughout the world, setting type in 900 different languages.

Other methods of mechanical composition came

This is a line of type which printers refer to as a slug.

along. One of them in 1897 was Tolbert Lanston's Monotype. This method is also still in use. Instead of making one line of type at a time as in Linotype, it made one piece of type at a time.

Yet these machines were only the start of the race to gather news, send it to the newspaper, print it, and get the papers on the newsstands. The Linotypes of today, and the newer Intertype machines, can be operated from a distance by a *teletypesetter* device.

When an exciting event takes place in a distant country, the reporter can telephone his story to the nearest teletypesetter operator; or if he is near enough, he can type the story himself on the machine. The message is tapped out on a special typewriter on a strip of *tape*. This tape, which makes holes instead of letters, is sent through a "sender," which sends electrical signals over the wire to a special machine attached to the Linotype in the newspaper office. This tape automatically operates the Linotype. Then in rapid succession the type is set, it goes to the pressroom, the giant presses begin to print, and within a few hours you are reading the very latest news from some far corner of the world.

All these inventions and improvements in the art

of printing brought on labor union difficulties. Printers at first objected to automation; they feared the new machines would do away with their jobs. But instead they found that automation created more jobs. They began to operate the new machines, to help build and repair them, to become printing salesmen, to move up to bigger and better jobs in the continually growing printing industry.

Yet, in spite of the new printing opportunities, many newspaper and magazine publishers were unable to meet the wage demands of labor unions and the constantly rising prices of paper and printing equipment. As a result, some publishers closed up the printting shop and went out of business.

But the world of printing will never go out of business. Even more marvelous inventions for the printing industry are in store for the future.

For example, there is the amazing voiceprinter or spectrogram. This machine records the vibrations of your voice—and no two voices are alike. It will eventually be combined with a printing machine.

Men are at work perfecting a computer that will feed coded tapes into machines that will set twelve

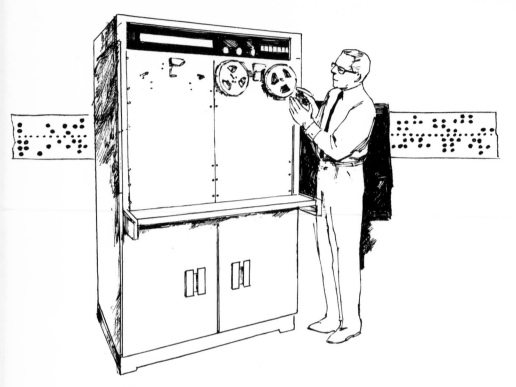

More and more methods of quickening the printing process are being discovered. This is an Intertype computer.

lines of type a minute.

Faster still is a machine that is expected to set a complete page, instead of a line, at a time.

The printing of tomorrow may be far different from the printing of today—just as today's newspa-

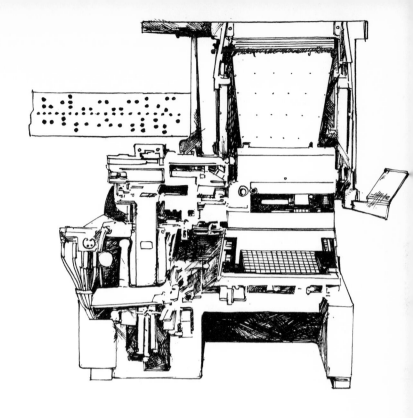

A Mergenthaler tape-operated linotype linecaster.

pers, magazines, and books are so different from the early pages turned out by Gutenberg.

We can only guess about the future. But one thing is certain. Printing, in whatever form, will always be with us, for people are always curious to learn more about the past, the present, and the future.

CHAPTER 9

How This Book "Happened"

Long before *Black on White and Read All Over* reached your hands, many exciting things had to happen. Let's suppose this book was your idea.

First, you have to go to several libraries and research the subject of printing. You read many books and make notes about its history, the inventions, and the men who made every step possible. Later you prepare an outline or brief plan, and from that you divide your proposed book into chapters.

Then you are ready to write the book. The double-spaced, typewritten pages are called a *manuscript*, or

Once the author has thoroughly researched his subject, he is ready to write his book.

"script" for short. Sometimes it takes several months or a year or longer to write a book. When it is finished, you send it to a book publishing company. The *editor* in the children's book department who reads the script likes it, and you sign a *contract* with the publishing company.

Now the editor takes over. She reads your script

carefully once again and suggests some changes, which you make. The editor has a *copyeditor* who checks your story for correct spelling, for punctuation, and who makes sure names, dates, and all facts are accurate.

Next the editor decides the format of the book: its shape and size, number of pages, illustrations, and whatever else will go into the book. This information is given to a *designer*, who chooses the type and plans how the manuscript and illustrations will fit together. An *artist* starts work on the illustrations and on the jacket of the book.

When all this is worked out, the manuscript, the design, and the illustrations are turned over to the *production department* to begin manufacturing your book.

Paper is ordered. The manuscript is sent to the compositor. He gives it to a Linotype operator, who sets the type which is printed on long narrow sheets of paper called *galley proofs*. You will receive a set of these galleys to read and to check for errors.

Meanwhile, the artist has finished his illustrations. A set of galleys and the illustrations are sent to the designer, who will prepare a *dummy*, a blank book that is the same size and number of pages as your book.

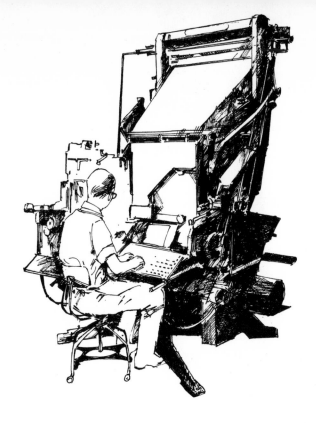

The linotype operator is setting type at the keyboard. As the slugs come from the machine, they are placed in long metal trays called galleys. Later, a proof of each galley is made. These proofs are known as galley proofs.

The designer is cutting the galleys into page lengths in order to paste them into the dummy.

The designer cuts the galleys into page lengths and pastes them into the dummy along with the illustrations, so the editor can see how the book will look.

If the dummy is approved, then the dummy, together with a set of corrected galleys, is sent to the production department.

From there the galleys go to the compositor to be

"broken" into pages. The pages, which are run off on special paper, are *reproduction proofs*. Using these proofs, an exact copy of the dummy is made. The pages of this new dummy are known as *mechanicals*. The mechanicals are sent to the printer who prepares them for reproduction by offset printing.

A section of a printing plant. The man at the left is inspecting the sheets as they come off the press.

While your book is being printed, the jacket is also going through various processes at the printer who specializes in this kind of printing.

Then, one day, the offset presses start to roll, and your book is printed on sheets of paper. Later the the sheets are folded, gathered, and bound together into a book. The paper jacket of your book is ready, too, and it is folded around the hard cover.

Thousands of copies of your book are printed to be bought by people all over the world. Yet the book is still not quite complete. It requires one more important ingredient—a reader. When a reader opens a book, interesting stories and exciting people from other places, lands, and times come alive. A rich treasure of knowledge and wisdom is mined. Centuries of history happen in a few hours of reading. What starts as a thought, is written down, printed, and finally read, perhaps touches the lives of millions of people. That is the magic and wonder of printing. It is a priceless tool that is absolutely necessary to build up and continue civilization's heritage of learning.

These printed sheets will be folded, gathered, and bound together into a book of the size shown in the pressman's hand.

Glossary

adjustable type mold—the mold invented by Gutenberg; it consists of two L-shaped pieces which form a box whose sides can be adjusted to fit the width of any letter, such as an I or W.

artist—there are many types of artists, but in the printing industry, he draws illustrations for books, magazines, and newspapers; such things as graphs and charts are also drawn by an artist.

automatic typesetting machine—invented by Mergenthaler. *See* Linotype.

automation—a system of setting type electronically by using teletypesetters, tapes, and computers; it is more accurate than older methods and requires much less operation by hand. *See also* tape; teletypesetter.

casting type—making type.

composing—the setting of type by a compositor. *See also* compositor.

composing room—a place at a newspaper office or at a printing plant where type is set.

compositor—a person who sets type; he can do this by many methods, such as Linotype or Monotype.

contract—a written agreement between an author and a publishing company; it contains such things as when a book will be published and how much the author will be paid.

copyeditor—a person who checks a manuscript for correct spelling, for punctuation, and to make sure names, dates, and all facts are accurate.

cylinder—part of a press that looks like a giant rolling pin. Cylinders carry paper, or the curved printing plates, or the rubber blanket.

designer—a person who chooses the style of type and who plans how the type and illustrations will fit together.

dummy—a blank book the same size and number of pages as the finished book. After the type has been set on long pieces of paper, called galleys, the galleys are cut into separate pages and pasted on blank pages. The illustrations are pasted in where they relate to the text. This is the dummy, and it directs the printer in making the final form of a book, magazine, or newspaper.

edition—all the copies of a book, newspaper, etc., printed just alike at the same time.

editor—a person who is in charge of all the things that have to be done to make a manuscript into a book, such as helping the author in writing the manuscript and deciding how the book should look; magazine and newspaper editors have the same sort of duties, but mainly they decide what articles should be published, and which ones should not.

etch—to make a design on a metal plate by using acid.

face—the style or cut of type; the part of metal type that imprints on the paper.

font—all characters (letters, numerals, etc.) of one size and
style of type.

foundry—a factory that makes type.

foundry type—a single letter made of hard metal and used
when setting type by hand.

galley proof—a long narrow sheet of paper on which the
type is first set; after all the corrections have been
marked on the galleys, they are sent back to the printer
who will reset the lines containing errors; then the type
is "broken" into pages and page proofs are made up.

impression—the printing of ink on paper by pressing the
inked surface against paper.

intaglio—a method of printing in which the design to be
printed lies below the surface of the plate; after the
plate has been inked, it is wiped clean so that only the ink
below the surface, in the design, remains; then a sheet
of paper is pressed down on the plate to pick up the ink
in the design.

Intertype—a machine similar to the Linotype. *See* Linotype.

letterpress—a method of printing in which raised surfaces on a block are inked and pressed onto paper; the lower surfaces, even if they have ink on them, do not reach the paper, and so they do not print on it. Also called relief printing.

Linotype—a machine with a keyboard, similar to that of a typewriter, that will automatically set a line of type when the keys for the various letters are punched.

lithography—a printing process in which the image to be printed is photographed and then reproduced onto a metal plate. (Originally, the image was drawn on stone.) The surface of the metal plate is treated so that the ink will stick to the image but not to the rest of the surface; when a piece of paper is pressed on the surface, the paper will pick up only the ink from the image.

manuscript—typewritten material prepared by an author; it will eventually be set in type and published, for example, as a magazine article or a story in a book.

mechanicals—an exact copy of the dummy that has been prepared using reproduction proofs.

mold—a small hollow box in which type is made.

Monotype—a machine that makes separate pieces of type and automatically assembles them to fill a single line.

movable type—pieces of type that can be rearranged and used over and over again.

offset lithography—a printing method in which the impression is made *indirectly*—from a plate to a rubber-covered cylinder, and from the rubber to the impression cylinder; the paper is printed as it passes between the rubber and impression cylinders.

plate—a sheet of metal on which the image to be printed is affixed.

photogravure—a process for making prints from an intaglio plate prepared by photographic methods.

pica—a printer's unit of measurement; one pica equals 1/6 of an inch.

point—a printer's unit of measurement; one point equals 1/72 of an inch.

relief printing—*See* letterpress.

reproduction proofs—the pages of the dummy that have been run off on special paper for photographic reproduction.

rotary press—a letterpress in which paper, fed from a continuous roll, is printed on as it passes between a cylinder holding type and a cylinder that presses the paper against the type.

rotogravure—a method of intaglio printing from copper cylinders in which the impression is produced by a rotary press.

sheet-fed—a press printing from individual sheets of paper.

spectrogram—*See* voiceprinter.

tape—perforated paper (that is, paper with small holes punched in it), in narrow rolls, which directs the action of automatic typesetters.

teletypesetter—a device for making perforated tape from a typewriter keyboard; the tape is used to send electrical signals over a wire to operate a Linotype automatically from some distance away.

type—a piece of metal that on one end has a raised letter, numeral, or some design that will print on paper when inked.

type case—a large, shallow drawer containing one font of type; type cases are usually stored in a cabinet, one case on top of another.

voiceprinter—a machine that records the vibrations of your voice; it will someday be combined with a printing machine.

web-fed—a press printing from a continuous roll of paper.

INDEX

A

Adjustable type mold, 17-18, 22
Allegheny Mountains, 39
Almanacs, 36-37
America, colonial, 31-39
America, United States of, 22, 39-41, 69
Arab traders, 12
Artists, 45, 54, 78
Asia/Asians, 12-14
Australia, 25
Automatic inking system, 63
Automatic typesetting machine, 67, 68
Automation, problems of, 72-73

B

Baskerville, John, 28-30
Bay Psalm Book, 32-33
Belgium, 22
Bible, the, 19-21, 29, 33, 41
Black on White and Read All Over, 50, 76-83
Bookmaking, 14-15, 28-30, 75-83
Book production, 76-83
Books, 14-15, 16, 18-22, 24, 25, 28-29, 31-33
Boston, Massachusetts, 33, 34
Bound books, 83
Bruges, Belgium, 24

C

Calico printing, 55
Canada, 25
Caslon, William, 27-28
Caxton, William, 24-25
China/Chinese, 8-12, 14, 42, 58
Chinese lamp black, 18, 43. *See also* Ink
Columbus, Christopher, 22
Composing stick, 65-66
Compositor, 65-67, 80-81
Constitution (United States), 39
Contract, 77
Copyeditor, 78
Currier and Ives, 45
Curved type plate, 46-47
Cut-in engraving. *See* Intaglio
Cutting type, 27. *See also* Type

D

Dampening roller, 47
Daumier, 45
Daye, Stephen, 32-33
Dayes, the, 32-33
Declaration of Independence, 27, 34
Delaware River, 34
Design, as an art, 14; cut-in (intaglio), 54-55; on metal, 16, 54-55; on stone, 43-45; type faces and, 27-30; wooden blocks and, 10-12

J

Jacket, book, 78, 83
Johnson (printer), 33

K

Keller (German weaver), 61
Klic, Karl, 55
Koenig, Frederick, 62-63

L

Lancaster, England, 55
Lanston, Tolbert, 72
Letterpress, 10-13, 18, 42, 51
Library of Congress, 21
Linen rags, in papermaking, 59
Linotype machine, 69-71, 72, 78
Lithographic prints, 45
Lithographs, color, 45
Lithography, 42-46, 51. *See also*
  Offset lithography
London, England, 24, 33

M

Mainz, Germany, 16, 21-22
Manuscript, 76-77, 78
Maps, 39-40
Massachusetts Bay Colony, 32
Mechanicals, 81-82
Mergenthaler, Ottmar, 68-71
Metals, 16, 17, 18, 54
Mexico City, 31-32
Mold, 17-18
Monotype, 72
Movable clay type, 12-14, 17
Movable metal type, 16-18, 22, 25-
  27. *See also* Type

Munich, Germany, 42

N

New England Courant, The, 34
Newspapers, 7, 25, 34-36, 37-39,
  39-41, 55, 57, 62-63, 67, 68, 69-
  75
New York, 25, 38
New York City, 33, 36, 38
New York Public Library, 33
New York Tribune, 69
New York Weekly Journal, The, 38
New Zealand, 25
Nile River, 9
North America, 32, 33
Nutley, New Jersey, 46

O

Offset, definition of, 47-48
Offset lithography, 47-53, 81, 83
Offset plates, making of, 52-53
Offset press (three cylinder), 47-49,
  50-53, 83
Oil and water, mixing of, 43-45, 46
Oral tradition, 23

P

Pablos, Juan, 31-32
Pages, 9, 18-19, 24, 26, 30, 74, 78,
  80-81
Paper, 7-9, 11-12, 15, 18, 22, 26-
  27, 28, 32, 41-42, 43, 46, 47-48,
  55, 58, 59-60, 61, 63, 64, 73, 78,
  83
Papermaking, 7-9, 12, 14-15, 16,
  58-62
Paper products, 7, 57

Papyrus, 9
Paris, France, 59
Pennsylvania, 34
Pennsylvania Gazette, The, 36
Philadelphia, Pennsylvania, 34, 36
Photogravure, 55. *See also*
   Rotogravure
Photo-offset, process of, 52-53. *See
   also* Offset lithography
Picas, 27
Pilgrims, 32
Pioneer printers, 39-41
Platemaking, intaglio, 54-55; letter-
   press, 10-13; photo-offset, 52-53;
   rotogravure, 56-59
Point, system of, 26-27, 29
Poor Richard's Almanac, 37
Posters, printed, 39-40
Power-driven presses, 63
Presses, 18-19, 22, 28, 31, 46-47,
   47-51, 55, 61-63, 72, 83
Printer's ink, 43-44
Printer's Union, 73
Printing, automatic typesetting and,
   68-72; automation of, 72-73;
   comes to America, 31-32; definition of, 9-10, 59-60; during colonial period, 33-39; first books,
   18-19; Gutenberg Bibles and, 19-
   22; importance of, 41, 85; in
   pioneer days, 39-41; lithography,
   42-46; offset lithography, 46-53;
   papermaking for, 58-62; press improvements for, 62-63; rotogravure, 54-59; type and, 24-29,
   64-69; spread of, 22-23.
Printshops, 20, 21, 24, 31, 34, 35
Production department, 78
Publishing company, 77

R

Raised surface printing, 10-12. *See
   also* Letterpress
Reid, Whitelaw, 69-71
Relief printing. *See* Letterpress
Reproduction proofs, 81-82
Revolution, American, 30, 39
Revolution, French, 59
Revolution, Printing, 58-67
Robert, Louis, 59
Roman type face, 63-64
Rotary press, 46-47, 55
Rotogravure, 55-57
Rubber blanket cylinder, 47-48
Rubel, Ira, 46-47

S

Sample page, 27
Saunders, Richard, 37
Screens, flat, 8-9; gravure, 56
Script. *See* Manuscript
Senefelder, Alois, 42-45, 46
Seville, Spain, 31
Sheet-fed press, 46
Silk, writing on, 8
Spain/Spanish, 12, 31-32
Spectrogram, 73
Stanhope, Charles, 61-62
Steam power, 62
Stone, lithographic, 43, 45-46
South America, 31, 32

T

Tapes, 72, 73-74
Teletypesetter, 72
Times, London, 62
Toulouse-Lautrec, 45